Dinosaur Book For Kids: From Compy to T-Rex

Speedy Publishing LLC
40 E. Main St. #1156
Newark, DE 19711

www.speedypublishing.com

Copyright 2015
9781681453309
First Printed January 28, 2015

Dino Facts...

Compsognathus, often referred to simply as "Compy", is a chicken-sized coelurosaurian dinosaur from the Late Jurassic Period (around 150 million years ago). It was first discovered in Germany before the only other specimen to be found was unearthed in France.

Dino Facts...

The longest dinosaur was Seismosaurus, which measured over 40 metres, as long as five double-decker buses. It was related to diplodocus, which for a long time held the honour.

Dino Facts...

The heaviest dinosaur was Brachiosaurus at 80 tonnes. It was the equivalent to 17 African Elephants. Brachiosaurus was 16m tall and 26m long and is the largest dinosaur skeleton to be mounted in a museum.

Dino Facts...

The smallest fully-grown fossil dinosaur is the little bird-hipped plant-eater like lesothosaurus, which was only the size of a chicken. Smaller fossilised examples have been found, but these are of baby dinosaurs.

Dino Facts...

One of the most intelligent dinosaurs was Troodon. It was a hunting dinosaur, about 2 metres long, and had a brain size similar to that of a mammal or bird of today, stereoscopic vision, and grasping hands.

Dino Facts...

Dinosaur eggs come in all shapes and sizes. They tend to be ovoid or spherical in shape and up to 30cm in length - about the size of a rugby ball. The smallest dinosaur egg so far found is only 3cm long. Once the egg has been fossilised it will become hard like rock, but it will retain a structure of its own.

Dino Facts...

Stegosaurus had a brain the size of a walnut - only 3 centimetres long and weighing 75 grams. However, comparing brain size to body size sauropodomorphs, like Plateosaurus, were probably one of the dumbest dinosaurs.

Dino Facts...

The tallest dinosaurs were the Brachiosaurid group of sauropods. Their front legs were longer than the rear legs giving them a giraffe-like stance. This combined with their extremely long necks, which were held vertically, meant they could browse off the tallest trees.

Dino Facts...

The speediest dinosaurs were the ostrich mimic ornithomimids, such as Dromiceiomimus, which could probably run at speeds of up to 60 kilometres per hour.

Dino Facts...

The oldest dinosaurs known are 230 million years old, and have been found in Madagascar. As yet they have not been formally named. Before this Eoraptor, meaning "dawn thief" had held the title at 228 million years.

Dino Facts...

**The dinosaur with
the longest name was
Micropachycephalosaurus
meaning "tiny thick-headed
lizard". Its fossils have been
found in China, and it was
named in 1978 by the Chinese
paleontologist Dong.**

Dino Facts...

Tyrannosaurus rex looked the most ferocious of all the dinosaurs, but in terms of overall cunning, determination and its array of vicious weapons it was Utahraptor that was probably the fiercest of all. Utahraptor measured about 7 metres, and was a very powerful, agile and intelligent predator.